A
Sorrow
Beyond
Dreams

A Sorrow Beyond Dreams

A LIFE STORY

Peter Handke

Translated by Ralph Manheim

A CONDOR BOOK
SOUVENIR PRESS (E&A) LTD

Printed in Great Britain by Fletcher & Son Ltd, Norwich
and bound by Richard Clay (The Chaucer Press), Ltd.,
Bungay, Suffolk.

He not busy being born is busy dying.

Bob Dylan

Dusk was falling quickly. It was just after 7 p.m., and the month was October.

Patricia Highsmith, *A Dog's Ransom*

A
Sorrow
Beyond
Dreams

The Sunday edition of the *Kärntner Volks-zeitung* carried the following item under "Local News": "In the village of A. (G. township), a housewife, aged 51, committed suicide on Friday night by taking an overdose of sleeping pills."

My mother has been dead for almost seven weeks; I had better get to work before the need to write about her, which I felt so strongly at her funeral, dies away and I fall back into the dull speechlessness with which I reacted to the news of her suicide. Yes, get to work: for, intensely as I sometimes feel the need to write about my mother, this need is so vague that if I didn't work at it I would, in my present state of mind, just sit at my typewriter pounding out the same letters over and over again. This sort of kinetic therapy alone would do me no good; it would only make me passive and apathetic. I might just as well take a trip—if I were traveling, my mindless dozing and lounging around wouldn't get on my nerves so much.

During the last few weeks I have been more irritable than usual; disorder, cold, and silence drive me to distraction; I can't see a bread crumb or a bit of fluff on the floor without bending down to pick it up. Thinking about this suicide, I become so insensible that I am sometimes startled to find that an object I have been holding hasn't fallen out of my hand. Yet I long for such moments, because they shake me out of my apathy and clear my head. My sense of horror makes me feel better: at last my boredom is gone; an unresisting body, no more exhausting distances, a painless passage of time.

The worst thing right now would be sympathy, expressed in a word or even a glance. I would turn away or cut the sympathizer short, because I need the feeling that what I am going through is incomprehensible and incommunicable; only then does the horror seem meaningful and real. If anyone talks to me about it, the boredom comes back, and everything is unreal again. Nevertheless, for no reason at all, I sometimes tell people about my mother's suicide, but if they dare to mention it I am furious. What I really want them to do is change the subject and tease me about something.

In his latest movie someone asks James Bond whether his enemy, whom he has just thrown over a stair rail, is *dead*. His answer—"Let's hope so!"—made me laugh with relief. Jokes about dying and being dead don't bother me at all; on the contrary, they make me feel good.

Actually, my moments of horror are brief, and what I feel is not so much horror as unreality; seconds later, the world closes in again, and if someone is with me I try to be especially attentive, as though I had just been rude.

Now that I've begun to write, these states seem to have dwindled and passed, probably because I try to describe them as accurately as possible. In describing them, I begin to remember them as belonging to a concluded period of my life, and the effort of remembering and formulating keeps me so busy that the short daydreams of the last few weeks have stopped. I look back on them as intermittent "states": suddenly my day-to-day world—which, after all, consists only of images repeated ad nauscam over a period of years and decades since they were new—fell apart, and my mind became so empty that it ached.

That is over now; I no longer fall into these states. When I write, I necessarily write about the past, about something which, at least while I am writing, is behind me. As usual when engaged in literary work, I am alienated from myself and transformed into an object, a remembering and formulating machine. I am writing the story of my mother, first of all because I think I know more about her and how she came to her death than any outside investigator who might, with the help of a religious, psychological, or sociological guide to the interpretation of dreams, arrive at a facile explanation of this interesting case of suicide; but second in my own interest, because having something to do brings me back to life; and lastly because, like an outside investigator, though in a different way, I would like to represent this VOLUNTARY DEATH as an exemplary case.

Of course, all these justifications are arbitrary and could just as well be replaced by others that would be equally arbitrary. In any case, I experienced moments of extreme speechlessness and needed to formulate them— the motive that has led men to write from time immemorial.

In my mother's pocketbook, when I arrived for the funeral, I found a post-office receipt for a registered letter bearing the number 432. On Friday afternoon, before going home and taking the sleeping pills, she had mailed a registered letter containing a copy of her will to my address in Frankfurt. (But why also SPECIAL DELIVERY?) On Monday I went to the same post office to telephone. That was two and a half days after her death. On the desk in front of the post-office clerk, I saw the yellow roll of registration stickers; nine more registered letters had been mailed over the weekend; the next number was 442, and this image was so similar to the number I had in my head that at first glance I became confused and thought for a moment nothing had happened. The desire to tell someone about it cheered me up. It was such a bright day; the snow; we were eating soup with liver dumplings; "it began with . . ."; if I started like this, it would all seem to be made up, I would not be extorting personal sympathy from my listener or reader, I would merely be telling him a rather fantastic story.

Well then, it began with my mother being born more than fifty years ago in the same village where she died. At that time all the land that was good for anything in the region belonged either to the church or to noble land-owners; part of it was leased to the population, which consisted mostly of artisans and small peasants. The general indigence was such that few peasants owned their land. For practical purposes, the conditions were the same as before 1848; serfdom had been abolished in a merely formal sense. My grandfather—he is still living, aged eighty-six—was a carpenter; in addition, he and his wife worked a few acres of rented farm and pasture land. He was of Slovenian descent and illegitimate. Most of the children born to small peasants in those days were illegitimate, because, years after attaining sexual maturity, few small peasants were in possession of living quarters or the means to support a household. His mother was the daughter of a rather well-to-do peasant, who, however, never regarded his hired man, my grandfather's father, as anything more than the "baby-maker." Nevertheless, my grandfather's mother inherited money enough to buy a small farm.

And so it came about that my grandfather was the first of his line—generations of hired men with blanks in their baptismal certificates, who had been born and who died in other people's houses and left little or no inheritance because their one and only possession, their Sunday suit, had been lowered into the grave with them—to grow up in surroundings where he could really feel at home and who was not merely tolerated in return for his daily toil.

Recently the financial section of one of our newspapers carried an apologia for the economic principles of the

Western world. Property, it said, was MATERIALIZED FREE-DOM. This may in his time have been true of my grand-father, the first in a long line of peasants fettered by poverty to own anything at all, let alone a house and a piece of land. The consciousness of owning something had so liberating an effect that after generations of will-lessness a will could now make its appearance: the will to become still freer. And that meant only one thing—jus-tifiably so for my grandfather in his situation—to enlarge his property, for the farm he started out with was so small that nearly all his labors went into holding on to it. The ambitious smallholder's only hope lay in saving.

So my grandfather saved, until the inflation of the twenties ate up all his savings. Then he began to save again, not only by setting aside unneeded money but also and above all by compressing his own needs and demand-ing the same frugality of his children as well; his wife, being a woman, had never so much as dreamed that any other way of life was possible.

He continued to save toward the day when his children would need SETTLEMENTS for marriage or to set them-selves up in a trade. The idea that any of his savings might be spent before then on their EDUCATION couldn't possibly have entered his head, especially where his daughters were concerned. And even in his sons the centuries-old dread of becoming a homeless pauper was so deeply in-grained that one of them, who more by accident than by design had obtained a scholarship to the Gymnasium, found those unfamiliar surroundings unbearable after

8

only a few days. He walked the thirty miles from the provincial capital at night, arriving home on a Saturday, which was house-cleaning day; without a word he started sweeping the yard: the noise he made with his broom in the early dawn told the whole story. He became a proficient and contented carpenter.

He and his older brother were killed early in the Second World War. In the meantime, my grandfather had gone on saving and once again lost his savings in the Depression of the thirties. His saving meant that he neither drank nor smoked, and played cards only on Sunday; but even the money he won in his Sunday card games—and he played so carefully that he almost always won—went into savings; at the most, he would slip his children a bit of small change. After the war, he started saving again; today he receives a government pension and is still at it.

The surviving son, a master carpenter with twenty workers in his employ, has no need to save. He invests, which means that he *can* drink and gamble; in fact, it's expected of him. Unlike his father, who all his life has been speechless and in every way self-denying, he has at least developed speech of a kind, though he uses it only in the town council, where he represents a small and obscure political party with visions of a grandiose future rooted in a grandiose past.

For a woman to be born into such surroundings was in itself deadly. But perhaps there was one comfort: no need to worry about the future. The fortune-tellers at our church fairs took a serious interest only in the palms of the young men; a girl's future was a joke.

No possibilities, it was all settled in advance: a bit of flirtation, a few giggles, brief bewilderment, then the alien, resigned look of a woman starting to keep house again, the first children, a bit of togetherness after the kitchen work, from the start not listened to, and in turn listening less and less, inner monologues, trouble with her legs, varicose veins, mute except for mumbling in her sleep, cancer of the womb, and finally, with death, destiny fulfilled. The girls in our town used to play a game based on the stations in a woman's life: Tired/Exhausted/Sick/Dying/Dead.

My mother was the next to last of five children. She was a good pupil; her teachers gave her the best possible marks and especially praised her neat handwriting. And then her school years were over. Learning had been a mere child's game; once your compulsory education was completed and you began to grow up, there was no need of it. After that a girl stayed home, getting used to the staying at home that would be her future.

No fears, except for an animal fear in the dark and in storms; no changes, except for the change between heat and cold, wet and dry, comfort and discomfort.

The passage of time was marked by church festivals, slaps in the face for secret visits to the dance hall, fits of envy directed against her brothers, and the pleasure of singing in the choir. Everything else that happened in the world was a mystery; no newspapers were read except the Sunday bulletin of the diocese, and then only the serial.

Sundays: boiled beef with horseradish sauce, the card game, the women humbly sitting there, a family photograph showing the first radio.

My mother was high-spirited; in the photographs she propped her hands on her hips or put her arm over her younger brother's shoulder. She was always laughing and seemed incapable of doing anything else.

Rain—sun; outside—inside: feminine feelings were very much dependent on the weather, because "outside" was seldom allowed to mean anything but the yard and "inside" was invariably the house, without a room of one's own.

The climate in that region is extremely variable: cold winters and sultry summers, but at sunset or even in the shade of a tree you shivered. Rain and more rain; from early September on, whole days of damp fog outside the tiny windows (they are hardly any larger today); drops of water on the clotheslines; toads jumping across your path in the dark; gnats, bugs, and moths even in the daytime; worms and wood lice under every log in the woodshed. You couldn't help becoming dependent on those things; there was nothing else. Seldom: desireless and somehow happy; usually: desireless and a little unhappy.

No possibility of comparison with a different way of life: richer? less hemmed in?

It began with my mother suddenly wanting something. She wanted to learn, because in learning her lessons as a child she had felt something of herself. Just as when we say, "I feel like myself." For the first time, a desire, and she didn't keep it to herself; she spoke of it time and time again, and in the end it became an obsession with her. My mother told me she had "begged" my grandfather to let her learn something. But it was out of the question, disposed of with a wave of the hand, unthinkable.

Still, our people had a traditional respect for accomplished facts: a pregnancy, a war, the state, ritual, and death. When at the age of fifteen or sixteen my mother ran away from home to learn cooking at some Hôtel du Lac, my grandfather let her have her own way, *because she was already gone;* and besides, there wasn't much to be learned about cooking.

No other course was open to her; scullery maid, chambermaid, assistant cook, head cook. "People will always eat." In the photographs, a flushed face, glowing cheeks, arm in arm with bashful, serious-looking girl friends; she was the life of the party; self-assured gaiety ("Nothing can happen to me"); exuberant, sociable, nothing to hide.

City life: short skirts ("knee huggers"), high-heeled shoes, permanent wave, earrings, unclouded joy of life. Even a stay abroad! Chambermaid in the Black Forest, flocks of ADMIRERS, kept at a DISTANCE! Dates, dancing, entertainment, fun; hidden fear of sex ("They weren't my type"). Work, pleasure; heavyhearted, lighthearted; Hitler had a nice voice on the radio. The homesickness of those who can't afford anything; back at the Hôtel du Lac ("I'm doing the bookkeeping now"); glowing references ("Fräulein . . . has shown aptitude and willingness to learn. So conscientious, frank, and cheerful that we find it hard . . . She is leaving our establishment of her own free will"). Boat rides, all-night dances, never tired.

On April 10, 1938, the Yes to Germany! "The Führer arrived at 4:15 p.m., after a triumphal passage through the streets of Klagenfurt to the strains of the Badenweiler March. The rejoicing of the masses seemed to know no bounds. The thousands of swastika flags in the spas and summer resorts were reflected in the already ice-free waters of the Wörthersee. The airplanes of the old Reich and our native planes vied with one another in the clouds overhead."

The newspapers advertised plebiscite badges and silk or paper flags. After football games the teams marched off with a regulation "Sieg Heil!" The letter A was replaced by the letter D on the bumpers of motor vehicles. On the radio: 6:15, call to arms; 6:35, motto of the day; 6:40, gymnastics; 8–12 p.m., Radio Königsberg: Richard Wagner concert followed by entertainment and dance music.

"How to mark your ballot on April 10: make a *bold* cross in the *larger* circle under the word YES."

Thieves just out of jail were locked up again when they claimed that the objects found in their possession had been bought in department stores that MEANWHILE HAD GONE OUT OF EXISTENCE because they had belonged to Jews.

Demonstrations, torchlight parades, mass meetings.

Buildings decorated with the new national emblem SA-
LUTED; forests and mountain peaks DECKED THEMSELVES
OUT; the historic events were represented to the rural
population as a drama of nature.

"We were kind of excited," my mother told me. For
the first time, people did things together. Even the daily
grind took on a festive mood, "until late into the night."
For once, everything that was strange and incomprehensible in the world took on meaning and became part of a
larger context; even disagreeable, mechanical work was
festive and meaningful. Your automatic movements took
on an athletic quality, because you saw innumerable
others making the same movements. A new life, in which
you felt protected, yet free.

The rhythm became an existential ritual. "Public need
before private greed, the community comes first." You
were at home wherever you went; no more homesickness.
Addresses on the backs of photographs; you bought your
first date book (or was it a present?)—all at once you had
so many friends and there was so much going on that it
became possible to FORGET something. She had always
wanted to be proud of something, and now, because what
she was doing was somehow important, she actually was
proud, not of anything in particular, but in general—a
state of mind, a newly attained awareness of being alive—
and she was determined never to give up that vague pride.

She still had no interest in politics: what was happening
before her eyes was something entirely different from politics—a masquerade, a newsreel festival, a secular church

fair. "Politics" was something colorless and abstract, not a carnival, not a dance, not a band in local costume, in short, nothing VISIBLE. Pomp and ceremony on all sides. And what was "politics"? A meaningless word, because, from your schoolbooks on, everything connected with politics had been dished out in catchwords unrelated to any tangible reality and even such images as were used were devoid of human content: oppression as chains or boot heel, freedom as mountaintop, the economic system as a reassuringly smoking factory chimney or as a pipe enjoyed after the day's work, the social system as a descending ladder: "Emperor–King–Nobleman–Burgher–Peasant–Weaver/Carpenter–Beggar–Gravedigger"; a game, incidentally, that could be played properly only in the prolific families of peasants, carpenters, and weavers.

That period helped my mother to come out of her shell and become independent. She acquired a presence and lost her last fear of human contact: her hat awry, because a young fellow was pressing his head against hers, while she merely laughed into the camera with an expression of self-satisfaction. (The fiction that photographs can "tell us" anything—but isn't all formulation, even of things that have really happened, more or less a fiction? *Less*, if we content ourselves with a mere record of events; *more*, if we try to formulate in depth? And the more fiction we put into a narrative, the more likely it is to interest others, because people identify more readily with formulations than with recorded facts. Does this explain the need for poetry? "Breathless on the riverbank" is one of Thomas Bernhard's formulations.)

The war—victory communiqués introduced by portentous music, pouring from the "people's radio sets," which gleamed mysteriously in dimly lit "holy corners"—further enhanced people's sense of self, because it "increased the uncertainty of all circumstances" (Clausewitz) and made the day-to-day happenings that had formerly been taken for granted seem excitingly fortuitous. For my mother the war was not a childhood nightmare that would color her whole emotional development as it did mine; more than anything else, it was contact with a fabulous world, hitherto known to her only from travel folders. A new feeling for distances, for how things had been BACK IN PEACETIME, and most of all for other individuals, who up until then had been confined to the shadowy roles of casual friends, dance partners, and fellow workers. And also for the first time, a family feeling: "Dear Brother . . . I am looking at the map to see where you might be now . . . Your sister . . ."

And in the same light her first love: a German party member, in civilian life a savings-bank clerk, now an army paymaster, which gave him a rather special standing. She was soon in a family way. He was married, and she loved him dearly; anything he said was all right with her. She introduced him to her parents, went hiking with him, kept him company in his soldier's loneliness.

"He was so attentive to me, and I wasn't afraid of him the way I had been with other men."

He did the deciding and she trailed along. Once he gave her a present—perfume. He also lent her a radio for her room and later took it away again. "At that time" he still read books, and together they read one entitled *By the Fireside*. On the way down from a mountain pasture on one of their hikes, they had started to run. My mother broke wind and my father reproved her; a little later he too let a fart escape him and followed it with a slight cough, hem-hem. In telling me of this incident years later, she bent double and giggled maliciously, though at the same time her conscience troubled her because she was belittling her only love. She herself thought it comical that she had once loved someone, especially a man like him. He was smaller than she, many years older, and almost bald; she walked beside him in low-heeled shoes, always at pains to adapt her step to his, her hand repeatedly slipping off his inhospitable arm; an ill-matched, ludicrous couple. And yet, twenty years later, she still longed to feel for someone what she had then felt for that savings-bank wraith. But there never was ANOTHER: everything in her life had conspired to inculcate a kind of love that remains fixated on a particular irreplaceable object.

It was after graduating from the Gymnasium that I first saw my father: on his way to the rendezvous, he chanced to come toward me in the street; he was wearing sandals,

17

a piece of paper was folded over his sunburned nose, and he was leading a collie on a leash. Then, in a small café in her home village, he met his former love; my mother was excited, my father embarrassed; standing by the juke-box at the other end of the café, I picked out Elvis Presley's "Devil in Disguise." My mother's husband had got wind of all this, but he had merely sent his youngest son to the café as an indication that he was in the know. After buying himself an ice-cream cone, the child stood next to his mother and the stranger, asking her from time to time, always in the same words, if she was going home soon. My father put sunglasses over his regular glasses, said something now and then to the dog, and finally announced that he "might as well" pay up. "No, no, it's on me," he said, when my mother also took her purse out of her handbag. On the trip we took together, the two of us wrote her a postcard. In every hotel we went to, he let it be known that I was his son, for fear we'd be taken for homosexuals (Article 175). Life had disappointed him, he had become more and more lonely. "Now that I know people, I've come to appreciate animals," he said, not quite in earnest of course.

Shortly before I was born, my mother married a German army sergeant, who had been COURTING her for some time and didn't mind her having a child by someone else. "It's this one or none!" he had decided the first time he laid eyes on her, and bet his buddies that he would get her or, conversely, that she would take him. She found him repulsive, but everyone harped on her duty (to give the child a father); for the first time in her life she let herself be intimidated and laughed rather less. Besides, it impressed her that someone should have taken a shine to her.

"Anyway, I figured he'd be killed in the war," she told me. "But then all of a sudden I started worrying about him."

In any case, she was now entitled to a family allotment. With the child she went to Berlin to stay with her husband's parents. They tolerated her. When the first bombs fell, she went back home—the old story. She began to laugh again, sometimes so loudly that everyone cringed.

She forgot her husband, squeezed her child so hard that it cried, and kept to herself in this house where, after the death of her brothers, those who remained looked uncomprehendingly through one another. Was there, then, nothing more? Had that been all? Masses for the dead, childhood diseases, drawn curtains, correspondence with old acquaintances of carefree days, making herself useful in the kitchen and in the fields, running out now and then to move the child into the shade; then, even here in the country, air-raid sirens, the population scrambling into the cave shelters, the first bomb crater, later used for children's games and as a garbage dump.

The days were haunted, and once again the outside

world, which years of daily contact had wrested from the nightmares of childhood and made familiar, became an impalpable ghost.

My mother looked on in wide-eyed astonishment. Fear didn't get the better of her; but sometimes, infected by the general fright, she would burst into a sudden laugh, partly because she was ashamed that her body had suddenly made itself so churlishly independent. In her childhood and even more so in her young girlhood, "Aren't you ashamed?" or "You ought to be ashamed!" had rung in her ears like a litany. In this rural, Catholic environment, any suggestion that a woman might have a life of her own was an impertinence: disapproving looks, until shame, at first acted out in fun, became real and frightened away the most elementary feelings. Even in joy, a "woman's blush," because joy was something to be ashamed of; in sadness, she turned red rather than pale and instead of bursting into tears broke out in sweat.

In the city my mother had thought she had found a way of life that more or less suited her, that at least made her feel good. Now she came to realize that, by excluding every other alternative, other people's way of life had set itself up as the one and only *hope of salvation*. When, in speaking of herself, she went beyond a statement of fact, she was silenced by a glance.

A bit of gaiety, a dance step while working, the humming of a song hit, were foolishness, and soon she herself thought so, because no one reacted and she was left alone with her gaiety. In part, the others lived their own lives as an example; they ate so little as an example, were silent in each other's presence as an example, and went to confession only to remind the stay-at-homes of their sins.

And so she was starved. Her little attempts to explain herself were futile mutterings. She felt free—but there was nothing she could do about it. The others, to be sure, were children; but it was oppressive to be looked at so reproachfully, especially by children.

When the war was over, my mother remembered her husband and, though no one had asked for her, went to Berlin. Her husband, who had also forgotten that he had once courted her on a bet, was living with a girl friend in Berlin; after all, there had been a war on.

But she had her child with her, and without enthusiasm they both took the path of duty.

They lived in a sublet room in Berlin-Pankow. The husband worked as a streetcar motorman and drank, worked as a streetcar conductor and drank, worked as a baker and drank. Taking with her her second child, who had been born in the meantime, his wife went to see his employer and begged him to give her husband one more chance, the old story.

In this life of misery, my mother lost her country-round cheeks and achieved a certain chic. She carried her head high and acquired a graceful walk. Whatever she put on was becoming to her. She had no need of fox furs. When her husband sobered up and clung to her and told her he loved her, she gave him a merciful, pitying smile. By then, she had no illusions about anything.

They went out a good deal, an attractive couple. When he was drunk, he got FRESH and she had to be SEVERE with him. Then he would beat her because she had nothing to say to him, when it was he who brought home the bacon.

Without his knowledge, she gave herself an abortion with a knitting needle.

For a time he lived with his parents; then they sent him back to her. Childhood memories: the fresh bread that he sometimes brought home; the black, fatty loaves of pumpernickel around which the dismal room blossomed into life; my mother's words of praise.

In general, these memories are inhabited more by things than by people: a dancing top in a deserted street amid ruins, oat flakes in a sugar spoon, gray mucus in a tin spittoon with a Russian trademark; of people, only separate parts: hair, cheeks, knotted scars on fingers; from her childhood days my mother had a swollen scar on her index finger; I held on to it when I walked beside her.

And so she was nothing and never would be anything; it was so obvious that there was no need of a forecast. She already said "in my day," though she was not yet thirty. Until then, she hadn't resigned herself, but now life became so hard that for the first time she had to listen to reason. She listened to reason, but understood nothing.

She had already begun to work something out and even, as far as possible, to live accordingly. She said to herself: "Be sensible"—the reason reflex—and "All right, I'll behave."

And so she budgeted herself and also learned to budget people and objects, though on that score there was little to be learned: the people in her life—her husband, whom she couldn't talk to, and her children, whom she couldn't yet talk to—hardly counted, and objects were available only in minimal quantities. Consequently, she became petty and niggardly: Sunday shoes were not to be worn on weekdays, street clothes were to be hung up as soon as you got home, her shopping bag wasn't a toy, the warm bread was for the next day. (Later on, my confirmation watch was locked up right after my confirmation.)

Because she was helpless, she disciplined herself, which went against her grain and made her touchy. She hid her touchiness behind an anxious, exaggerated dignity, but at the slightest provocation a defenseless, panic-stricken look shone through. She was easily humiliated.

Like her father, she thought the time had come to deny herself everything, but then with a shamefaced laugh she would ask the children to let her lick their candy.

The neighbors liked her and admired her for her Austrian sociability and gaiety; they thought her FRANK and SIMPLE, not coquettish and affected like city people; there was no fault to be found with her.

She also got on well with the Russians, because she could make herself understood in Slovenian. With them she talked and talked, saying everything she was able to say in the words common to both languages; that unburdened her.

But she never had any desire for an affair. Her heart had grown heavy too soon: the shame that had always been preached at her and finally become a part of her. An affair, to her mind, could only mean someone "wanting something" of her, and that put her off; she, after all, didn't want anything of anybody. The men she later liked to be with were GENTLEMEN: their company gave her a pleasant feeling that took the place of affection. As long as there was someone to talk with, she felt relaxed and almost happy. She let no one come too close; she could have been approached only with the delicacy which in former days had enabled her to feel that she belonged to herself—but that was long ago; she remembered it only in her dreams.

She became sexless; everything went into the trivia of daily life.

She wasn't lonely; at most, she sensed that she was only a half. But there was no one to supply the other half. "We rounded each other out so well," she said, thinking back on her days with the savings-bank clerk; that was her ideal of eternal love.

The postwar period; the big city—in this city, city life was no longer possible. You took shortcuts, up hill and down dale through the rubble, to get there sooner, but even so you found yourself at the end of a long line, jostled by fellow citizens who had ceased to be anything more than elbows and eyes looking into space. A short, unhappy laugh; like the rest of them, you looked away from yourself, into space; like the rest of them, you gave yourself away, showed that you needed something; still, you tried to assert yourself; pathetic, because that made you just like the people around you: something pushing and pushed, shoving and shoved, cursing and cursed at. In her new situation, her mouth, which up until then had been open at least occasionally—in youthful amazement (or in feminine acting-as-if), in rural fright, at the end of a daydream that lightened her heavy heart—was kept closed with exaggerated firmness, as a sign of adaptation to a universal determination which, because there was so little to be *personally* determined about, could never be more than a pretense.

A masklike face—not rigid as a mask but with a masklike immobility—a disguised voice, which for fear of attracting attention not only spoke the foreign dialect but mimicked the foreign turns of phrase—"Mud in your eye!"—"Keep your paws off that!"—"You're sure shoveling it in today!"—a copied posture, with a bend at the hips and one foot thrust forward . . . all this in order to become, not a different person, but a TYPE: to change from a prewar type to a postwar type, from a country bumpkin to a city person, adequately described in the words: TALL, SLIM, DARK-HAIRED.

In thus becoming a type, she felt freed from her own

25

history, because now she saw herself through the eyes of a stranger making an erotic appraisal.

And so an emotional life that never had a chance of achieving bourgeois composure acquired a superficial stability by clumsily imitating the bourgeois system of emotional relations, prevalent especially among women, the system in which "So-and-so is my type but I'm not his," or "I'm his but he's not mine," or in which "We're made for each other" or "can't stand the sight of each other"—in which clichés are taken as binding rules and any *individual* reaction, which takes some account of an actual person, becomes a deviation. For instance, my mother would say of my father: "Actually, he wasn't my type." And so this typology became a guide to life; it gave you a pleasantly objective feeling about yourself; you stopped worrying about your origins, your possibly dandruff-ridden, sweaty-footed individuality, or the daily renewed problem of how to go on living; being a type relieved the human molecule of his humiliating loneliness and isolation; he lost himself, yet now and then he was somebody, if only briefly.

Once you became a type, you floated through the streets, buoyed up by all the things you could pass with indifference, repelled by everything which, in forcing you to stop, brought you back bothersomely to yourself: the lines outside the shops, a high bridge across the Spree, a shop window with baby carriages in it. (She had given herself another secret abortion.) Always on the move to get away from yourself and keep your peace of mind. Motto: "Today I won't think of anything; today I'll enjoy myself."

At times it worked and everything personal was swallowed up by the typical. Then even sadness was only a passing phase, a suspension of good cheer: "Forsaken, forsaken, / Like a pebble in the street, / That's how forsaken I am"; with the foolproof melancholy of this phony folk song, she contributed her share to the general merriment; the next item on the program might, for instance, be the ribald tone of a male voice getting ready to tell a joke. And then, with a sense of release, you could join in the laughter.

At home, of course, she was alone with the FOUR WALLS; some of the bounce was still there, a hummed tune, a dance step while taking off her shoes, a brief desire to jump out of her skin. And then she was dragging herself around the room again, from husband to child, from child to husband, from one thing to another.

Her calculations always went wrong; the little bourgeois recipes for salvation had stopped working, because in actual fact her living conditions—the one-room apartment, the constant worry about where the next meal was coming from, the fact that communication with her LIFE COMPANION was confined almost exclusively to gestures, involuntary mimicry, and embarrassed sexual intercourse—were actually pre-bourgeois. It was only by leaving the house that she could get anything at all out of life. Outside: the victor type; inside: the weaker half, the eternal loser! What a life!

Whenever she told me about it later on—and *telling* about it was a need with her—she would shake with disgust and misery, but too feebly to shake them *off*; her shudders only revived her horror.

From my childhood: ridiculous sobs in the toilet, nose blowing, inflamed eyes. She was; she became; she became nothing.

(Of course what is written here about a particular person is rather general; but only such generalizations, in explicit disregard of my mother as a possibly unique protagonist in a possibly unique story, can be of interest to anyone but myself. Merely to relate the vicissitudes of a life that came to a sudden end would be pure presumption.

(The danger of all these abstractions and formulations is of course that they tend to become independent. When that happens, the individual that gave rise to them is forgotten—like images in a dream, phrases and sentences enter into a chain reaction, and the result is a literary ritual in which an individual life ceases to be anything more than a pretext.

(These two dangers—the danger of merely telling what happened and the danger of a human individual becoming painlessly submerged in poetic sentences—have slowed down my writing, because in every sentence I am afraid of losing my balance. This is true of every literary effort, but especially in this case, where the facts are so overwhelming that there is hardly anything to think out.

(Consequently, I first took the facts as my starting point and looked for ways of formulating them. But I soon noticed that in looking for formulations I was moving away from the facts. I then adopted a new approach—starting not with the facts but with the already available formulations, the linguistic deposit of man's social experience. From my mother's life, I sifted out the elements that were already foreseen in these formulas, for only with the help of a ready-made public language was it possible to single out from among all the irrelevant facts of this life the few that cried out to be made public.

(Accordingly, I compare, sentence by sentence, the stock of formulas applicable to the biography of a woman with my mother's particular life; the actual work of writing follows from the agreements and contradictions between them. The essential is to avoid mere quotations; even when sentences look quoted, they must never allow one to forget that they deal with someone who to my mind at least is distinct. Only then, only if a sentence is firmly and circumspectly centered on my personal or, if you will, private subject, do I feel that I can use it.

(Another specific feature of this story is that I do not, as is usually the case, let every sentence carry me further away from the inner life of my characters, so as finally, in a liberated and serene holiday mood, to look at them

from outside as isolated insects. Rather, I try with unbending earnestness to penetrate my character. And
because I cannot fully capture her in any sentence, I keep
having to start from scratch and never arrive at the usual
sharp and clear bird's-eye view.

(Ordinarily, I start with myself and my own headaches;
in the course of my writing, I detach myself from them
more and more, and then in the end I ship myself and my
headaches off to market as a commodity—but in this case,
since I am only a *writer* and can't take the role of the
person written about, such detachment is impossible. I
can only move myself into the distance; my mother can
never become for me, as I can for myself, a wingèd art
object flying serenely through the air. She refuses to be
isolated and remains unfathomable; my sentences crash
in the darkness and lie scattered on the paper.

(In stories we often read that something or other is
"unnamable" or "indescribable"; ordinarily this strikes
me as a cheap excuse. This story, however, is really about
the nameless, about speechless moments of terror. It is
about moments when the mind boggles with horror,
states of fear so brief that speech always comes too late;
about dream happenings so gruesome that the mind
perceives them physically as worms. The blood curdles,
the breath catches, "a cold chill crept up my back, my
hair stood on end"—states experienced while listening to
a ghost story, while turning on a water faucet that you
can quickly turn off again, on the street in the evening
with a beer bottle in one hand; in short, it is a record of

states, not a well-rounded story with an anticipated, hence comforting, end.

(At best, I am able to capture my mother's story for brief moments in dreams, because then her feelings become so palpable that I experience them as doubles and am identical with them; but these are precisely the moments I have already mentioned, in which extreme need to communicate coincides with extreme speechlessness. That is why I affect the usual biographical pattern and write: "At that time . . . later," "Because . . . although," "was . . . became . . . became nothing," hoping in this way to dominate the horror. That, perhaps, is the comical part of my story.)

In the early summer of 1948, my mother left the eastern sector of Germany with her husband and two children, carrying the little girl, who was just a year old, in a shopping bag. They had no papers. They crossed two borders illegally, both in the gray of dawn; once a Russian border guard shouted "Halt," and my mother's answer in Slovenian served as a password; those days became fixed in the boy's mind as a triad of gray dawn, whispers, and danger. Happy excitement on the train ride through Austria, and then she was back in the house where she was born, where two small rooms were turned over to her and her family. Her husband was employed as foreman by her carpenter brother; she herself was reincorporated into the household.

In the city she had not been proud of having children; here she was, and often showed herself with them. She no longer took any nonsense from anyone. In the old days her only reaction had been a bit of back talk; now she laughed. She could laugh anyone to silence. Her husband, in particular, got laughed at so vigorously whenever he started discussing his numerous projects that he soon faltered and looked vacantly out the window. True, he would start in again the next day. (That period lives for me in the sound of my mother laughing at people!) She also interrupted the children with her laughter when they wanted something; it was ridiculous to express desires in earnest. In the meantime, she brought her third child into the world.

She took to the native dialect again, though of course only in fun: she was a woman who had been ABROAD. Almost all her old girl friends had by then returned to their native village; they had made only brief excursions to the city or across the borders.

In this life, confined almost entirely to housekeeping and making ends meet, you didn't confide in your friends; at the most, friendship meant familiarity. It was plain from the start that all had the same troubles—the only difference was that some took them more lightly than others, a matter of temperament.

In this section of the population, people without troubles were an oddity—freaks. Drunks didn't get talkative, only more taciturn; they might bellow or brawl for a while, but then they sank back into themselves, until at closing time they would start sobbing for no known reason and hug or thrash whoever was nearest to them.

No one had anything to say about himself; even in church, at Easter confession, when at least once a year there was an opportunity to reveal something of oneself, there was only a mumbling of catchwords out of the catechism, and the word "I" seemed stranger to the speaker himself than a chunk out of the moon. If in talking about himself anyone went beyond relating some droll incident, he was said to be "peculiar." Personal life, if it had ever developed a character of its own, was depersonalized except for dream tatters swallowed up by the rites of religion, custom, and good manners; little remained of the human individual, and indeed, the word "individual" was known only in pejorative combinations.

The sorrowful Rosary; the glorious Rosary; the harvest festival; the plebiscite celebration; ladies' choice; the drinking of brotherhood; April Fools' pranks; wakes; kisses on New Year's Eve: in these rituals all private sorrow, ambition, hunger for communication, sense of the unique, wanderlust, sexual drive, and in general all reactions to a lopsided world in which the roles were reversed, were projected outward, so that no one was a problem to himself.

All spontaneity—taking a walk on a weekday, falling in love a second time, or, if you were a woman, going to the tavern by yourself for a schnapps—was frowned upon; in a pinch you could ask someone to dance or join in a song "spontaneously," but that was all. Cheated out of your own biography and feelings, you became "skittish"; you shied away from people, stopped talking, or, more seriously touched, went from house to house screaming.

The above-mentioned rites then functioned as a consolation. This consolation didn't address itself to you as a person; it simply swallowed you up, so that in the end you as an individual were content to be nothing, or at least nothing much.

You lost interest in personal matters and stopped inquiring about them. All questions became empty phrases, and the answers were so stereotyped that there was no need to involve *people* in them; *objects* sufficed; the cool grave, the sweet heart of Jesus, the sweet Lady of Sorrows, became fetishes for the death wish that sweetened your daily afflictions; in the midst of these consoling fetishes, you ceased to exist. And because your days were spent in unchanging association with the same things, they became sacred to you; not leisure but work was sweet. Besides, there was nothing else.

You no longer had eyes for anything. "Curiosity" ceased to be a human characteristic and became a womanish vice.

But my mother was curious by nature and had no consoling fetishes. Instead of losing herself in her work, she took it in her stride; consequently she was discontented. The *Weltschmerz* of the Catholic religion was alien to her; she believed only in happiness in this world, and that was a matter of luck; she herself had had bad luck.

She'd still show them, though.

But how?

How she would have loved to be really frivolous! And then she actually did something frivolous: "I've been frivolous today, I've bought myself a blouse." All the same—and that was a good deal in those surroundings—she took to smoking and even smoked in public.

Many of the local women were secret drinkers; their thick, twisted lips repelled her: that wasn't the way to show them. At the most she would get tipsy, and then she would drink to lifelong friendship with everyone in sight, and soon she was on friendly terms with all the younger notables. Even in this little village there was a kind of "society," consisting of the few who were somewhat better off than the rest, and she was welcome in their gatherings. Once, disguised as a Roman matron, she won first prize at a masked ball. At least in its merrymaking, country society thought of itself as classless—as long as you were NEAT, CLEAN, and JOLLY.

At home she was "Mother"; even her husband addressed her as "Mother" more often than by her first name. That was all right with her; for one thing, it corresponded to her feeling about her husband: she had never regarded him as anything resembling a sweetheart.

Now it was she who saved. Her saving, to be sure, could not, like her father's, mean setting money aside. It was pure *scrimping;* you curtailed your needs to the point where they became vices, and then you curtailed them some more.

But even in this wretchedly narrow sphere, she comforted herself with the thought that she was at least imitating the *pattern* of middle-class life: ludicrous as it might seem, it was still possible to classify purchases as necessary, merely useful, and luxurious.

Only food was necessary; winter fuel was useful; everything else was a luxury.

If only once a week, she derived a pleasurable feeling of pride from the fact that a little something was left over for luxury. "We're still better off than the rest of them."

She indulged in the following luxuries: a seat in the ninth row at the movies, followed by a glass of wine and soda water; a one- or two-schilling bar of Bensdorp chocolate to give the children the next morning; once a year, a bottle of homemade eggnog; on occasional winter Sundays she would whip up the cream she had saved during the week by keeping the milk pot between the two panes of the double windows overnight. "What a feast!" I would write if it were my own story; but it was only the slavish aping of an unattainable life style, a child's game of earthly paradise.

Christmas: necessities were packaged as presents. We surprised each other with such necessities as underwear, stockings, and handkerchiefs, and the beneficiary said he had WISHED for just that! We pretended that just about everything that was given to us, except food, was a present; I was sincerely grateful for the most indispensable school materials and spread them out beside my bed like presents.

A budgeted life, determined by the hourly wages she totted up for her husband, always hoping to discover a forgotten half hour; dread of rainy spells, when the wages were next to nothing, which he passed in their little room talking to her or looking resentfully out the window.

In the winter, when there was no building, her husband spent his unemployment benefits on drink. She went from tavern to tavern looking for him; with gleeful malice, he would show her what was left. She ducked to avoid his blows. She stopped talking to him. The children, repelled and frightened by her silence, clung to their contrite father. Witch! The children looked at her with hostility; she was so stern and unbending. They slept with pounding hearts when their parents were out and pulled the blanket over their heads when toward morning the husband pushed the wife into the room. At every step she stopped until he pushed her. Both were obstinately mute. Then finally she opened her mouth and said what he had been waiting to hear: "You beast! You beast!" whereupon he was able to beat her in earnest. To every blow she responded with a short, crushing laugh.

They seldom looked at each other except in these moments of open hatred; then they looked deep and unflinchingly into each other's eyes, he from below, she from above. The children under the blanket heard only the shoving and breathing, and occasionally the rattling of dishes in the cupboard. Next morning they made their own breakfast while husband and wife lay in bed, he dead to the world, she with her eyes closed, pretending to be asleep. (Undoubtedly, this kind of account seems copied, borrowed from accounts of other incidents; an old story interchangeable with other old stories; unrelated to the time when it took place; in short, it smacks of the nineteenth century. But just that seems necessary, for, at least in that part of the world and under the given economic conditions, such anachronistic, interchangeable nineteenth-century happenings were still the rule. And even today the Town Hall bulletin board is taken up almost entirely by notices to the effect that So-and-so and So-and-so are forbidden to enter the taverns.)

She never ran away. She had learned her place. "I'm only waiting for the children to grow up." A third abortion, this time followed by a severe hemorrhage. Shortly before she was forty, she became pregnant again. An abortion was no longer possible; the child was born.

The word "poverty" was a fine, somehow noble word. It evoked an image out of old schoolbooks: poor but clean. Cleanliness made the poor socially acceptable. Social progress meant teaching people to be clean; once the indigent had been cleaned up, "poverty" became a title of honor. Even in the eyes of the poor, the squalor of destitution applied only to the filthy riffraff of foreign countries.

"The tenant's visiting card is his windowpane."

And so the have-nots obediently bought soap with the money provided for that purpose by the progressive authorities. As paupers, they had shocked the official mind with repulsive, but for that very reason palpable, images; now, as a reclaimed and cleansed "poorer class," their life became so unimaginably abstract that they could be forgotten. Squalid misery can be described in concrete terms; poverty can only be intimated in symbols.

Moreover, the graphic accounts of squalor were concerned only with its physically disgusting aspect; they *produced* disgust by the relish they took in it, so that disgust, instead of being translated into action, merely became a reminder of the anal, shit-eating phase.

In certain households, for instance, there was only one bowl; at night it was used as a chamberpot and by day for kneading bread dough. Undoubtedly the bowl was washed out with boiling water in between, so there was little harm done; the dual use of the bowl became disgusting only when it was *described*: "They relieve themselves in the same bowl they eat out of."—"Ugh!" Words convey this sort of passive, complacent disgust much better than the sight of the phenomena they refer to. (A memory of my own: shuddering while describing spots of egg yolk

39

on a dressing gown.) Hence my distaste for descriptions of misery; for in hygienic, but equally miserable, poverty, there is nothing to describe.

Accordingly, when the word "poverty" comes up, I always think: "once upon a time"; and, for the most part, one hears it in the mouth of persons who have gone through it in the past, a word connected with childhood; not "I was poor" but "I was the child of poor parents" (Maurice Chevalier): a quaint note to season memoirs with. But at the thought of my mother's living conditions, I am unable to embroider on my memory. From the first, she was under pressure to keep up the forms: in country schools, the subject most stressed for girls was called "the outward form and appearance of written work"; in later life, this found its continuation in a woman's obligation to keep up the appearance of a united family; not cheerful poverty but formally perfect squalor; and gradually, in its daily effort to keep up appearances, her face lost its soul.

Maybe we would have felt better in formless squalor; we might have achieved a degree of proletarian class-consciousness. But in that part of the world there was no proletariat, at most, beggars and tramps; no one fought or even talked back; the totally destitute were merely embarrassed; poverty was indeed a disgrace.

Nevertheless, my mother, who had not learned to take all this for granted, was humiliated by the eternal stringency. In symbolic terms: she was no longer a NATIVE WHO HAD NEVER SEEN A WHITE MAN; she was capable of imagining a life that was something more than lifelong housework. If someone had given her the slightest hint, she would have got the right idea.

If, would have.

What actually happened: a nature play with a human prop that was systematically dehumanized. Pleading with her brother not to dismiss her husband for drunkenness; pleading with the local radio spotter not to report her unregistered radio; pleading with the bank for a building loan, protesting that she was a good citizen and would prove worthy of it; from office to office for a certificate of indigence, which had to be renewed each year if her son, who was now at the university, was to obtain a scholarship; applications for sick relief, family allowances, reduction of church taxes—most of which depended on the benevolent judgment of the authorities, but even if you had a legal right to something, you had to prove it over and over again in such detail that when the "Approved" stamp finally came, you received it with gratitude, as a favor.

No machines in the house; everything was still done by hand. Objects out of a past century, now generally transfigured with nostalgia: not only the coffee mill, which you had actually come to love as a toy—also the GOOD OLD ironing board, the COZY hearth, the often-mended cooking pots, the DANGEROUS poker, the STURDY wheelbarrow, the ENTERPRISING weed cutter, the SHINING BRIGHT knives, which over the years had been ground to a vanishing narrowness by BURLY scissors grinders, the FIENDISH thimble, the STUPID darning egg, the CLUMSY OLD flatiron, which provided variety by having to be put back on the stove every so often, and finally the PRIZE PIECE, the foot- and hand-operated Singer sewing machine. But the golden haze is all in the manner of listing.

Another way of listing would be equally idyllic: your aching back; your hands scalded in the wash boiler, then frozen red while hanging up the clothes (how the frozen washing crackled as you folded it up!); an occasional nosebleed when you straightened up after hours of bending over; being in such a hurry to get through with the day's work that you went marketing with that telltale blood spot on the back of your skirt; the eternal moaning about little aches and pains, because after all you were only a woman. Women among themselves: not "How are you feeling?" but "Are you feeling better?"

All that is known. It proves nothing; its demonstrative value is destroyed by the habit of thinking in terms of advantages and disadvantages, the most evil of all ways of looking at life. "Everything has its advantages and disadvantages." Once that is said, the unbearable becomes bearable—a mere disadvantage, and what after all is a disadvantage but a necessary adjunct of every advantage?

An advantage, as a rule, was merely the absence of a

disadvantage: *no* noise, *no* responsibility, *not* working for strangers, *not* having to leave your house and children every day. The disadvantages that were absent made up for those that were present.

So it wasn't really so bad; you could do it with one hand tied behind your back. Except that no end was in sight.

Today was yesterday, yesterday was always. Another day behind you, another week gone, and Happy New Year. What will we have to eat tomorrow? Has the mailman come? What have you been doing around the house all day?

Setting the table, clearing the table: "Has everybody been served?" Open the curtains, draw the curtains; turn the light on, turn the light out; "Why do you always leave the light on in the bathroom?"; folding, unfolding; emptying, filling; plugging in, unplugging. "Well, that does it for today."

The first electrical appliance: an iron, a marvel she had "always longed for." Embarrassment, as though she had been unworthy of it: "What have I done to deserve it? From now on I'll always look forward to ironing! Maybe I'll have a little more time for myself."

The mixer, the electric stove, the refrigerator, the washing machine: more and more time for herself. But she only stood there stiff with terror, dizzy after her long years as the good household fairy. But she had also had to husband her feelings so much that she expressed them only in slips of the tongue, and then did her best to gloss them over. The animal spirits that had once filled her whole body now showed themselves only seldom; one finger of her heavy, listless hand would quiver, and instantly this hand would be covered by the other.

But my mother had not been crushed for good. She began to assert herself. No longer obliged to work her fingers to the bone, she gradually became herself again. She got over her skittishness. She showed people the face with which she felt more or less at ease.

She read newspapers, but preferred books with stories that she could compare with her own life. She read the books I was reading, first Fallada, Knut Hamsun, Dostoevsky, Maxim Gorky, then Thomas Wolfe and William Faulkner. What she said about books could not have been put into print; she merely told me what had particularly caught her attention. "I'm not like that," she sometimes said, as though the author had written about *her*. To her, every book was an account of her own life, and in reading she came to life; for the first time, she came out of her shell; she learned to talk about her*self*; and with each book she had more ideas on the subject. Little by little, I learned something about her.

Up until then she had got on her own nerves, her own presence had made her uncomfortable; now she lost herself in reading and conversation, and emerged with a new feeling about herself. "It's making me young again."

True, books to her were only stories out of the past, never dreams of the future; in them she found everything she had missed and would never make good. Early in life she had dismissed all thought of a future. Thus, her second spring was merely a transfiguration of her past experience.

Literature didn't teach her to start thinking of herself but showed her it was too late for that. She COULD HAVE made something of herself. Now, at the most, she gave SOME thought to herself, and now and then after shopping she would treat herself to a cup of coffee at the tavern and worry a LITTLE LESS about what people might think.

She became indulgent toward her husband; when he started talking, she let him finish; she no longer stopped him after the first sentence with a nod so violent that it made him swallow his words. She felt sorry for him; often her pity left her defenseless when he wasn't suffering at all and she merely thought of him in connection with some object which to her mind stood for her own past despair: a washbasin with cracked enamel, a tiny electric hot plate, blackened by boiled-over milk.

When a member of the family was absent, she surrounded him with images of loneliness; if he wasn't at home with her, he was sure to be alone. Cold, hunger, unfriendly people: and it was all her fault. She included her despised husband in these guilt feelings and worried about him when he had to manage without her; even during her frequent stays at the hospital, once on suspicion of cancer, her conscience tormented her: her poor husband at home wasn't getting anything hot to eat.

Her sympathy for him when he was absent prevented her from ever feeling lonely; only a brief moment of forsakenness when she had him on her hands again; the irrepressible distaste inspired by his wobbly knees and the drooping seat of his trousers. "If only I had a man I could look up to"; it was no good having to despise someone all the time.

This visible disgust in her very first gesture, attenuated over the years into a patient, polite looking-up from whatever she happened to be doing, only crushed him the more. She had always thought him WEAK-KNEED. He often made the mistake of asking her why she couldn't bear him. Invariably she answered: "What makes you think that?" He persisted: was he really so repulsive? She comforted him, and all the while her loathing grew. They were growing old together; the thought didn't move her, but on the surface it made life easier, because he got out of the habit of beating her and bullying her.

Exhausted by the daily labors that got him nowhere, he became sickly and gentle. He woke from his maunderings into a real loneliness, to which she could respond only in his absence.

They hadn't grown apart; they had never been really together. A sentence from a letter: "My husband has calmed down." And she lived more calmly beside him, drawing satisfaction from the thought that she had always been and always would be a mystery to him.

She began to take an interest in politics; she no longer voted like her husband, for his employer's and her brother's party. Now she voted Socialist; and after a while her husband, who felt an increasing need to lean on her, did so too. But she never believed that politics could be of any help to her personally. She cast her ballot as a gift, never expecting anything in return. "The Socialists do more for the workers"—but she didn't feel herself to be a worker.

The preoccupations that meant more and more to her, as housekeeping took up less of her time, had no place in what she knew of the Socialist system. She remained alone with her sexual disgust, repressed till it found an outlet only in dreams, with the fog-dampened bedclothes and the low ceiling over her head. The things that really mattered to her were not political. Of course there was a flaw in her reasoning—but what was it? And what politician could explain it to her? And in what words?

Politicians lived in another world. When you asked them a question, they didn't answer; they merely stated their positions. "You can't talk about most things anyway." Politics was concerned only with the things that could be talked about; you had to handle the rest for yourself, or leave it to God. And besides, if a politician were

47

to take an interest in you personally, you'd bolt. That would be getting too intimate.

She was gradually becoming an individual.

Away from the house, she took on an air of dignity; sitting beside me as I drove the secondhand car I had bought her, she looked unsmilingly straight ahead. At home she no longer bellowed when she sneezed, and she didn't laugh as loudly as before.

(At her funeral, her youngest son was to remember how on his way home in those days he had heard her, while still a long way off, screaming with laughter.)

When shopping, she dispensed token greetings to the right and left; she went to the hairdresser's more often and had her nails manicured. This was no longer the assumed dignity with which she had run the gantlet in the days of postwar misery—today no one could destroy her composure with a glance.

But sometimes at home, while her husband, his back turned to her, his shirttails hanging out, his hands thrust deep into his pockets, silent except for an occasional suppressed cough, gazed down into the valley and her youngest son sat snotnosed on the kitchen sofa reading a Mickey Mouse comic book, she would sit at the table in her new, erect posture, angrily rapping her knuckles on the table edge, and then suddenly raise her hand to her cheek. At this her husband, as often as not, would leave the house, stand outside the door for a while clearing his throat, and come in again. She sat there with her hand on her cheek until her son asked for a slice of bread with something on it. To stand up she had to prop herself on both hands.

Another son wrecked the car and was thrown in jail for driving without a license. Like his father, he drank, and again she went from tavern to tavern. What a brood! He paid no attention to her reproofs, she always said the same thing, she lacked the vocabulary that might have had some effect on him. "Aren't you ashamed?"—"I know," he said.—"You could at least get yourself a room somewhere else."—"I know." He went on living at home, duplicated her husband, and even damaged the next car. She packed his bag and put it outside the house; he left the country. She dreamed the worst about him, wrote him a letter signed "Your unhappy mother," and he came right back. And so on. She felt that she was to blame. She took it hard.

And then the always identical objects all about her, in always the same places! She tried to be untidy, but her daily puttings-away had become too automatic. If only she could die! But she was afraid of death. Besides, she was too curious. "I've always had to be strong; I'd much rather have been weak."

She had no hobbies; she didn't collect anything or

swap anything. She had stopped doing crossword puzzles. She had given up pasting photographs in albums; she just put them away somewhere.

She took no part in public life; once a year she gave blood and wore the blood donor's badge on her coat. One day she was introduced on the radio as the hundred thousandth donor of the year and rewarded with a gift basket.

Now and then she went bowling at the new automatic bowling alley. She giggled with her mouth closed when the tenpins all toppled over and the bell rang.

Once, on the Heart's Desire radio program, relatives in East Berlin sent the whole family greetings, followed by Handel's Hallelujah Chorus.

She dreaded the winter, when they all spent their days in one room; no one came to see her; when she heard a sound and looked up, it was always her husband again: "Oh, it's you."

She began having bad headaches. She couldn't keep pills down; at first suppositories helped, but not for long. Her head throbbed so that she could only touch it, ever so gently, with her fingertips. Each week the doctor gave her an injection that eased the pain for a while. But soon the injections became ineffectual. The doctor told her to keep her head warm, and she went about with a scarf on her head. She took sleeping pills but usually woke up soon after midnight; then she would cover her face with her pillow. She lay awake trembling until it was light, and the trembling lasted all day. The pain made her see ghosts.

In the meantime her husband had been sent to a sanatorium with tuberculosis; he wrote affectionate letters, he begged her to let him lie beside her again. Her answers were friendly.

The doctor didn't know what was wrong with her; the usual female trouble? change of life?

She was so weak that often when she reached out for something, she missed her aim; her hands hung down limp at her sides. After washing the lunch dishes, she lay down awhile on the kitchen sofa; it was too cold in the bedroom. Sometimes her headache was so bad that she didn't recognize anyone. Nothing interested her. When her head was throbbing, we had to raise our voices to talk to her. She lost all sense of balance and orientation, bumped into the corners of things, and fell down stairs. It hurt her to laugh, she only grimaced now and then. The doctor said it was probably a strangulated nerve. She hardly spoke above a whisper, she was even too miserable to complain. She let her head droop, first on one side, then on the other, but the pain followed her.

"I'm not human any more."

Once, when staying with her summer before last, I found her lying on her bed with so wretched a look on her face that I didn't dare go near her. A picture of animal misery, as in a zoo. It was a torment to see how shamelessly she had turned herself inside out; everything about her was dislocated, split, open, inflamed, a tangle of entrails. And she looked at me from far away as if I were her BROKEN HEART, as Karl Rossmann was for the humiliated stoker in Kafka's novel. BROKEN HEART. Frightened and exasperated, I left the room.

Only since then have I been fully aware of my mother. Before that, I kept forgetting her, at the most feeling an occasional pang when I thought about the idiocy of her life. Now she imposed herself on me, took on body and reality, and her condition was so palpable that at some moments it became a part of me.

The people in the neighborhood also began to see her with other eyes; as though she had been chosen to bring their own lives home to them. They still asked why and wherefore, but only on the surface; they understood her without asking.

↙

She became insensible, she couldn't remember anything or recognize even the most familiar objects. More and more often, when her youngest son came home from school, he found a note on the table saying she had gone out, he should make himself some sandwiches or go next door to eat. These notes, torn from an account book, piled up in the drawer.

She was no longer able to play the housewife. Her whole body was sore when she woke up in the morning.

She dropped everything she picked up, and would gladly have followed it in its fall.

Doors got in her way; the mold seemed to rain from the walls as she passed.

She watched television but couldn't follow. She moved her hands this way and that to keep from falling asleep.

Sometimes in her walks she forgot herself. She sat at the edge of the woods, as far as possible from the houses, or beside the brook below an abandoned sawmill. Looking at the grain fields or the water didn't take away her pain but deadened it intermittently. Her feelings dovetailed with the things she looked at; every sight was a torment; she would turn to another, and that too would torment her. But in between there were dead points, when the whirligig world left her a moment's peace. At such moments, she was merely tired; thoughtlessly immersed in the water, she rested from the turmoil.

Then again everything in her clashed with the world around her; panic-stricken, she struggled to keep her balance, but the feeling was too strong and her peace was gone. She had to stand up and move on.

She had to walk very slowly because, as she told me, the horror strangled her.

She walked and walked until she was so tired she had to sit down again. But soon she had to stand up and go on.

So the time passed, and often she failed to notice that it was getting dark. She was night-blind and had difficulty in finding her way home. Outside the house, she stopped and sat down on a bench, afraid to go in.

Then, after a long while, the door opened very slowly and my mother stood there with vacant eyes, like a ghost.

But in the house as well she wandered about, mistaking doors and directions. Often she had no idea how she had come to be where she was or how the time had passed. She had lost all sense of time and place.

She lost all desire to see anyone; at the most she would sit in the tavern, among the people from the tourist buses, who were in too much of a hurry to look her in the face. She couldn't dissemble any more; she had put all that behind her. One look at her and anyone was bound to see what was wrong.

She was afraid of losing her mind. Quickly, for fear it would be too late, she wrote a few letters of farewell.

Her letters were full of urgency, as if she had tried to etch herself into the paper. In that period of her life, writing had ceased to be an extraneous effort, as it is for most people in her circumstances; it had become a reflex, independent of her will. Yet there was hardly anything one could talk to her about; every word reminded her of some horror and threw her off balance. "I can't talk. Don't torture me." She turned away, turned again, turned further away. Then she had to close her eyes, and silent tears ran uselessly down her averted face.

She went to see a neurologist in the provincial capital. With him she could talk; a doctor was someone she could confide in. She herself was surprised at how much she told him. It was only in speaking that she began really to remember. The doctor nodded at everything she said, recognized every particular as a symptom, and by subsuming them under a name—"nervous breakdown"— organized them into a system. That comforted her. He knew what was wrong with her; at least he had a name for her condition. And she wasn't the only one; there were others in the waiting room.

On her next visit, it amused her to observe these people. The doctor advised her to take walks in the open air. He prescribed a medicine that somewhat relieved the pressure on her head. A trip would help, she needed a change. On each visit she paid cash, because the Workers Health Insurance didn't provide for treatment of this kind. And then she was depressed again, because of the expense.

Sometimes she searched desperately for a word for something. Usually she knew it, she merely wanted others to share in her thought. She looked back with nostalgia at the brief period when she had recognized no one and understood nothing.

As it wore off, her illness became an affectation; now she only played at being sick. She pretended that her head was in a muddle as a defense against her thoughts, which had become clear again; for, once her head was perfectly clear, she could only regard herself as an individual case and the consolation of belonging to a group was no longer available to her. She exaggerated her forgetfulness and absent-mindedness in order to be encouraged, when she finally did remember or show that she had understood everything perfectly, with a "You see! You're much better now!"—as though all the horror had consisted in losing her memory and being unable to join in the conversation.

🖎

You couldn't joke with her. Teasing about her condition didn't help her. SHE TOOK EVERYTHING LITERALLY. If anyone started clowning to cheer her up, she burst into tears.

🖎

In midsummer she went to Yugoslavia for four weeks. At first she only sat in her darkened hotel room, touching and feeling her head. She couldn't read, her thoughts got in the way. Every few minutes she went to the bathroom and washed her hands and face.

Then she ventured out and dabbled in the water. This was her first vacation away from home and her first visit to the seashore. She liked the sea; at night there was often a storm, and then she didn't mind lying awake. She bought a straw hat to shield her from the sun and sold it back the day she left. Every afternoon she went to a café and ordered an espresso. She wrote cards and letters to all her friends in which she spoke only incidentally of herself.

She recovered her sense of time and awareness of her surroundings. She listened curiously to the conversations at the other tables and tried to figure out the relationships between the people.

Toward evening when the heat had let up she took walks; she went to villages nearby and looked into the doorless houses. Her amazement was real; she had never seen such dire poverty. Her headaches stopped and so did her thoughts. For a time she was outside the world. She felt pleasantly bored.

Back home, she was her old talkative self. She had plenty to talk about. She let me go with her on her walks. Now and then we went to the tavern for dinner and she got into the habit of drinking a Campari before her meal. She still clutched at her head, but by then it was little more than a tic. She remembered that a year ago a man had actually spoken to her in a café. "But he was very polite!" Next summer she thought she would go to some northern country where it wasn't so hot.

She took it easy, sat in the garden with her friends, smoking and fanning the wasps out of her coffee.

The weather was sunny and mild. The fir trees on the hills round about were veiled in mist all day, and for a time they were not as dark as usual. She put up fruit and vegetables for the winter, and thought of adopting a child.

🖎

I was already too busy with my own life. In the middle of August, I went back to Germany and left her to her own resources. During the following months I was working on a book. I heard from her occasionally.

"My head spins a little. Some days are hard to bear."

57

"It's cold and cheerless, the fog doesn't lift until mid-morning. I sleep late, and when I finally crawl out of bed, I have no desire to do anything. And adopting a child is out of the question right now. They won't give me one because my husband has tuberculosis."

"Whenever a pleasant thought crops up, a door closes and I'm alone again with my nightmares. I'd be so glad to write something more cheerful, but there isn't anything. When I start a conversation, he doesn't know what I'm talking about, so I prefer to say nothing. Somehow I was looking forward to seeing him again, but when he's here I can't bear the sight of him. I know I ought to find some way of making life bearable, I keep thinking about it, but nothing occurs to me. Just read this and forget it as fast as you can, that's my advice."

"I can't stand it in the house any more, so I'm always gadding about somewhere. I've been getting up a little earlier, that's the hardest time for me; I have to force myself to do something, or I'd just go back to bed. There's a terrible loneliness inside me, I don't feel like talking to anyone. I'd often like to drink a little something in the evening, but I mustn't, because if I did my medicine wouldn't take effect. Yesterday I went to Klagenfurt, I roamed around all day and caught the last local home."

In October she didn't write. During the fine autumn days someone would meet her walking slowly down the street and prod her to walk a little faster. She was always asking her friends to join her in a cup of coffee at the tavern. People invited her out on Sunday excursions and she was glad to go. She went with friends to the last church fairs of the year. Sometimes she even went to a football game. She would look on indulgently as her friends cheered and whistled, and hardly open her mouth. But when in the course of his re-election campaign the Chancellor stopped in the village and handed out carnations, she pushed boldly through the crowd and asked for one: "Haven't you got one for me?" "I beg your pardon, ma'am."

Early in November she wrote: "I'm not logical enough to think things through to the end, and my head aches. Sometimes it buzzes and whistles so that I can't bear any outside noise.

"I talk to myself, because I can't say anything to other people any more. Sometimes I feel like a machine. I'd like to go away somewhere, but when it gets dark I'm afraid of not finding the way home again. In the morning there's a dense fog and then everything is so quiet. Every day I do the same work, and every morning the place is a mess again. There's never any end to it. I really wish I were dead. When I'm out in the street and I see a car coming, I want to fall in front of it. But how can I be sure it would work?

59

"Yesterday I saw Dostoevsky's 'The Gentle Spirit' on TV; all night long I saw the most gruesome things, I wasn't dreaming, I really saw them, some men were going around naked and instead of genitals they had intestines hanging out. My husband is coming home on December 1. I keep feeling more and more uneasy. I can't see how it will be possible to live with him. We each look in a different direction and the loneliness only gets worse. I'm cold now, I think I'll take a walk."

She often shut herself up in the house. When people started telling her their troubles, she stopped them short. She treated them all very harshly, silenced them with a wave of her hand or with her sudden laugh. Other people were irritating children; at best she felt slightly sorry for them.

She was often cross. There was something about her way of finding fault that often made people feel like hypocrites.

When her picture was taken, she was no longer able to compose her face. She puckered her forehead and raised her cheeks in a smile, but there was an incurable sadness in her eyes; her pupils were out of kilter, displaced from the center of her irises.

Mere existence had become a torture to her.

But at the same time she had a horror of death.

"Take walks in the woods!" (The neurologist.)

"But it's dark in the woods!" the local veterinarian, her

occasional confidant, said contemptuously after her
death.

Day and night the fog hung on. At noon she tried putting
the light out and immediately turned it on again. What
should she look at? Cross her arms and put her hands on
her shoulders. From time to time, an invisible buzz saw,
a rooster who thought all day that the day was just dawn-
ing and crowed until late afternoon; and then at closing
time the factory whistles.

At night the fog pressed against the windowpanes. At
irregular intervals she could hear a drop of water running
down the glass outside. She kept the heating pad on all
night in her bed. Every morning the fire was out in the
kitchen stove. "I don't want to pull myself together any
more." She was no longer able to close her eyes. There
had been a GREAT FALL (Franz Grillparzer) in her consciousness.

(From this point on, I shall have to be careful to keep my
story from telling itself.)

She wrote letters of farewell to everyone in her family.
She not only knew what she was doing, she also knew
why she could no longer do anything else. "You won't
understand," she wrote to her husband. "But it's unthink-

able that I should go on living." To me she wrote a registered special-delivery letter, enclosing a copy of her will. "I have begun to write several times, but it's no comfort, no help to me." All her letters were headed not only with the date as usual but also with the day of the week: "Thursday, November 18, 1971."

The next day she took the local to the district capital and had the prescription our family doctor had given her refilled: a hundred sleeping pills. Though it was not raining, she also bought a red umbrella with a handsome, slightly curved, wooden handle.

Late that afternoon she took the local back. As a rule this train is almost empty. She was seen by one or two people. She went home and ate dinner at the house next door, where her daughter was living. Everything as usual: "We even told jokes."

Then, in her own house, she watched television with her youngest son. A movie from the Father and Son series was being shown.

She sent the child to bed; the television was still playing. She had been to the hairdresser's the day before and had had her nails done. She turned off the television, went to her bedroom, and hung up her brown two-piece dress in the wardrobe. She took all the sleeping pills and all her antidepression pills. She put on menstrual pants, stuffed diapers inside, put on two more pairs of pants and an ankle-length nightgown, tied a scarf under her chin, and lay down on the bed. She did not turn on the heating pad. She stretched out and laid one hand on the other. At the end of her letter to me, which otherwise contained only instructions for her funeral, she wrote that she was perfectly calm, glad at last to be falling asleep in peace. But I'm sure that wasn't true.

🖋

The following afternoon, on receiving the news of her death, I flew to Austria. The plane was half empty; it was a steady, quiet flight, the air clear and cloudless, the lights of changing cities far below. Reading the paper, drinking beer, looking out the window, I gradually sank into a tired, impersonal sense of well-being. Yes, I thought over and over again, carefully enunciating my thoughts to myself: THAT DOES IT. THAT DOES IT. THAT DOES IT. GOOD. GOOD. GOOD. And throughout the flight I was beside myself with pride that she had committed suicide. Then the plane prepared to land and the lights grew larger and larger. Dissolved in a boneless euphoria against which I was powerless, I moved through the almost deserted airport building. In the train the next morning, I listened to a woman who was one of the Vienna Choirboys' singing teachers. Even when they grew up, she was telling her companion, the Choirboys were unable to stand on their own feet. She had a son who was one of them. On a tour in South America, he was the only one who had managed on his pocket money. He had even brought some of it back. She had reason to hope that he, at least, would

63

have some sense when he grew up. I couldn't stop
listening.

I was met at the station and driven home in the car. Snow
had fallen during the night; now it was cloudless, the sun
was shining, it was cold, the air sparkled with frost. What
a contradiction to be driving through a serenely civilized
countryside—in weather that made this countryside so
much a part of the unchanging deep-blue space above it
that no further change seemed thinkable—to a house of
mourning and a corpse that might already have begun to
rot! During the drive I was unable to get my bearings or
form a picture of what was to come, and the dead body in
the cold bedroom found me utterly unprepared.

Chairs had been set up in a row and women sat drinking
the wine that had been served them. I sensed that little
by little, as they looked at the dead woman, they began to
think of themselves.

The morning before the funeral I was alone in the room
with the body for a long while. At first my feelings were
at one with the custom of the deathwatch. Even her dead
body seemed cruelly forsaken and in need of love. Then I
began to be bored and looked at the clock. I had decided
to spend at least an hour with her. The skin under her
eyes was shriveled, and here and there on her face there
were still drops of holy water. Her belly was somewhat
bloated from the effect of the pills. I compared the hands

on her bosom with a fixed point at the end of the room to make sure she was not breathing after all. The furrow between her nose and upper lip was gone. Sometimes, after looking at her for a while, I didn't know what to think. At such moments my boredom was at its height and I could only stand distraught beside the corpse. When the hour was over, I didn't want to leave; I stayed in the room beyond the time I had set myself.

Then she was photographed. From which side did she look best? "The sugar-side of the dead."

The burial ritual depersonalized her once and for all, and relieved everyone. It was snowing hard as we followed her mortal remains. Only her name had to be inserted in the religious formulas. "Our beloved sister . . ." On our coats candle wax, which was later ironed out.

It was snowing so hard that you couldn't get used to it; you kept looking at the sky to see if it was letting up. One by one, the candles went out and were not lighted again. How often, it passed through my mind, I had read of someone catching a fatal illness while attending a funeral.

The woods began right outside the graveyard wall. Fir woods on a rather steep hill. The trees were so close together that you could see only the tops of even the second row, and from then on treetops after treetops. The people left the grave quickly. Standing beside it, I looked up at the motionless trees: for the first time it seemed to me that nature was really merciless. So these were the facts! The forest spoke for itself. Apart from these countless treetops nothing counted; in the foreground, an episodic jumble of shapes, which gradually receded from the picture. I felt mocked and helpless. All at once, in my impotent rage, I felt the need of writing something about my mother.

In the house that evening I climbed the stairs. Suddenly I took several steps at one bound, giggling in an unfamiliar voice, as if I had become a ventriloquist. I ran up the last few steps. Once upstairs I thumped my chest lustily and hugged myself. Then slowly, with a sense of self-importance, as though I were the holder of a unique secret, I went back down the stairs.

It is not true that writing has helped me. In my weeks of preoccupation with the story, the story has not ceased to preoccupy me. Writing has not, as I at first supposed, been a remembering of a concluded period in my life, but merely a constant pretense at remembering, in the form of sentences that only lay claim to detachment. Even now I sometimes wake up with a start, as though in response to some inward prodding, and, breathless with horror, feel that I am literally rotting away from second to second. The air in the darkness is so still that, losing their balance, torn from their moorings, the things of my world fly soundlessly about: in another minute they will come crashing down from all directions and smother me. In these tempests of dread, I become magnetic like a decaying animal and, quite otherwise than in undirected pleasure, where all my feelings play together freely, I am attacked by an undirected, objective horror.

Obviously narration is only an act of memory; on the other hand, it holds nothing in reserve for future use; it merely derives a little pleasure from states of dread by trying to formulate them as aptly as possible; from enjoyment of horror it produces enjoyment of memory.

Often during the day I have a sense of being watched. I open doors and look out. Every sound seems to be an attempt on my life.

Sometimes, of course, as I worked on my story, my frankness and honesty weighed on me and I longed to write something that would allow me to lie and dissemble a bit, a play, for instance.

Once, when I was slicing bread, my knife slipped; instantly, I remembered how in the morning she used to cut thin slices of bread and pour warm milk on them for the children.

Often, as she passed by, she would quickly wipe out the children's ears and nostrils with her saliva. I always shrank back from the saliva smell.

Once, while mountain climbing with a group of friends, she started off to one side to relieve herself. I was ashamed of her and started to bawl, so she held it in.

In the hospital she was always in a big ward with a lot of other people. Yes, those things still exist! Once in such a hospital ward she pressed my hand for a long while.

When everyone had been served and had finished eating, she would daintily pop the remaining scraps into her mouth.

(These, of course, are anecdotes. But in this context scientific inferences would be just as anecdotal. All words and phrases are too mild.)

The eggnog bottle in the sideboard!

My painful memory of her daily motions, especially in the kitchen.

When she was angry, she didn't beat the children; at the most, she would wipe their noses violently.

Fear of death when I wake up at night and the light is on in the hallway.

Some years ago I had the idea of making an adventure movie with all the members of my family; it would have had nothing to do with me personally.

As a child, she was moonstruck.

She died on a Friday, and during the first few weeks it was on Fridays that her death agony was most present to me. Every Friday the dawn was painful and dark. The yellow streetlights in the night mist; dirty snow and sewer smell; folded arms in the television chair; the last toilet flushing, twice.

Often while at work on my story I felt that writing music would be more in keeping with its incidents. Sweet New England . . .

"Perhaps there are new, unsuspected kinds of despair that are unknown to us," said a village schoolmaster in a crime-thriller series. *The Commissar*.

All the jukeboxes in the region had a record titled WORLD-WEARY POLKA.

The first signs of spring—mud puddles, warm wind, and snowless trees. Far away, far beyond my typewriter.

"She took her secret with her to the grave."

In one dream she had a second face, but it too was rather worn.

She was kindly.

Then again, something cheerful: in a dream I saw all sorts of things that were intolerably painful to look at. Suddenly someone came along and in a twinkling took the painful quality out of all these things. LIKE TAKING DOWN AN OUT-OF-DATE POSTER. The metaphor was part of my dream.

One summer day I was in my grandfather's room, looking out the window. There wasn't much to be seen: a street led uphill through the village to a building that was painted dark ("Schönbrunn") yellow, an old-time inn; there it turned off to one side. It was a SUNDAY AFTER-NOON, the street was DESERTED. All at once, I had a bitter-tasting feeling for the man who lived in that room; I felt that he would soon die. But this feeling was softened by the knowledge that his death would be a natural one.

Horror is something perfectly natural: the mind's horror vacui. A thought is taking shape, then suddenly it notices that there is nothing more to think. Whereupon it crashes to the ground like a figure in a comic strip who suddenly realizes that he has been walking on air.

Someday I shall write about all this in greater detail.

Written January–February 1972